POCKET

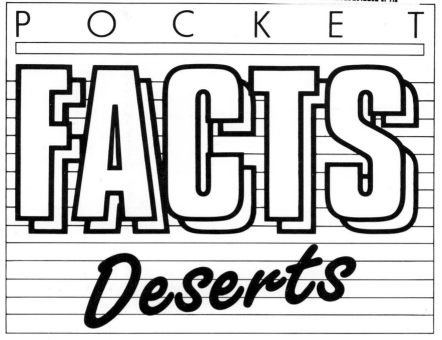

FACTS

Deserts

Philip Steele

HEINEMANN

What is a desert?

The term 'desert' can be used to describe any wilderness or wasteland. It normally refers to an area where there is very little moisture and poor soil, such as sand, gravel or rock. Because of this, there are few plants to offer shelter or shade. Deserts are harsh places. Many are burning hot by day and cold by night. Some are cold deserts, in which snow sprinkles the sand. The Kara Kum Desert (right) is in the USSR.

Where are the deserts?

The world's biggest desert is the Sahara, which occupies 9.1 million square kilometres of North Africa. Other large deserts include the Namib and Kalahari of southwest Africa, the Australian Desert, the Great American and the Atacama Deserts of the Americas, and the Gobi, Thar and Arabian Deserts of Asia. The explorers (below) are setting up camp in Egypt's Sinai Peninsula.

The heat of the day

Death Valley (right) lies to the north of the Mojave Desert in the United States. It is a desolate world of rock and sand, in which the temperature can reach 50°C. The highest temperature ever recorded is 58°C in the shade, in the Libyan part of the Sahara. Humans cannot stand such heat, and many people die in hot deserts. Most hot deserts have less than 25 centimetres of rainfall in a year. At night, hot deserts cool rapidly.

The cold desert

The Gobi Desert (below) stretches across northern China and Mongolia. In winter, snows from Siberia cover the sands, and the temperature has been known to drop to -50°C. The Bactrian or two-humped camels that live there have thick coats to keep warm. The summer temperatures in this region can soar to 48°C.

How are deserts formed?

Lands which are far from the sea often have very dry climates, as the winds pick up little moisture. In some areas a range of mountains acts as a barrier to rain-bearing winds. A desert forms behind the mountains (below). Some deserts may even form near the sea, in areas where there are few winds to carry rainfall.

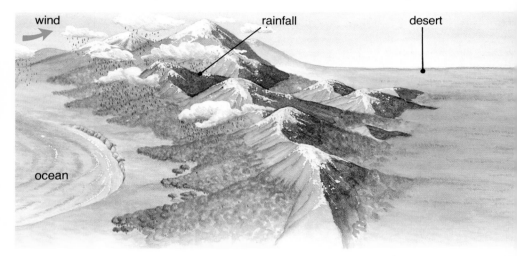

What are dunes?

Deserts have few plants, so little moisture is trapped. There are no roots to hold soil in place. The wind blasts the rock and over the ages wears it down. Tiny pieces of rocks such as quartz form sand. The sand is blown in the wind, causing dust storms. Sand piles up in huge banks called dunes (right). These can be 400 metres high. They constantly shift with the wind.

4

What are wadis?

In some deserts it may not rain for years on end. When it does, there may be a sudden and violent storm. Water may fall on dry soil that is as hard as concrete. Dry valleys called wadis (right) soon fill up with a rushing torrent of water. People and animals may be swept away by these sudden or flash floods.

Rain brings life to the desert. Some seeds remain in the soil for years until the rains make them sprout.

Desert rocks

Wind and water have shaped desert landscapes over thousands of years. Rivers carrying sand and grit have carved out deep valleys, called canyons. In the American state of Arizona the Colorado River has cut a gorge 349 kilometres long, 24 kilometres wide and two kilometres deep. This is the Grand Canyon.

The Great American Desert has some of the most fantastic rock formations on Earth. The wind has blasted the rocks with sand. Soft rocks have been worn away, leaving the hard cores as tall pillars (right). Heat and cold also shape desert landscapes, cracking and crumbling rocks. The way in which rocks are worn away by the weather is called erosion.

What are oases?

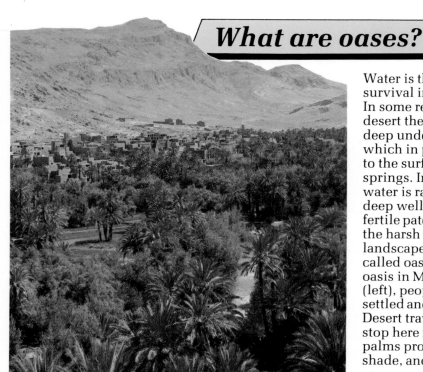

Water is the key to survival in the desert. In some regions of the desert there is water deep underground, which in places comes to the surface in springs. In others, the water is raised from deep wells. Here green, fertile patches appear in the harsh desert landscape. They are called oases. At this oasis in Morocco (left), people have settled and built homes. Desert travellers can stop here for a rest. Date palms provide food and shade, and a few other crops can be grown.

Rivers in the desert

In some places wide rivers flow through desert regions. The Nile (right) is such a large river that it never dries up. In Egypt its waters are led off along small channels into the fields. This irrigation makes it possible to grow crops. The soil is rich, because for thousands of years floods have left river mud along the banks. However the green banks of the Nile only form a narrow strip. On either side, burning sands stretch into the distance. Without the Nile, Egypt would be nothing more than desert.

What are water holes?

Oases are settlements built in the deserts around supplies of water. At other places in the desert there may be smaller springs and wells. These water holes may not be large enough to support a settlement or crops, but they provide a lifeline for desert travellers and their herds. In the Thar Desert of north-west India (right), sheep, goats and camels are brought to these water holes to drink. Wild animals may also visit the water holes.

Keeping alive

Living things need water to stay alive. If we do not drink, our bodies dry up. They become dehydrated. In hot deserts we lose a lot of water by sweating. We need to drink at least 5.5 litres of water a day. The peoples who live in deserts have found many ways of obtaining liquid to drink. Some suck the juices of cactus and other plants. The San people of the Kalahari can find hidden pockets of water under the sand. They suck it up through reeds (right) and store it in ostrich shells until it is needed.

When the desert flowers

In order to grow, plants need sunshine, soil and water. In deserts there is a great deal of sunshine, but only poor soil and not enough water. Even so, many plants have managed to survive in these conditions. Flowering plants must have very tough seeds. The seeds are covered by a thick coating which protects them over long, dry periods. When the first rains come, they wash off the coating, and further showers make the seeds sprout. Many desert plants are protected from water loss by tiny hairs or by a waxy coating on the leaves and stem. Others are partly buried in the sand, to protect them from the sun. Some deserts are covered with carpets of flowers after a period of rain. Tough trees also grow in some deserts, such as the Joshua trees of the American deserts, and the acacias and thorns of Africa.

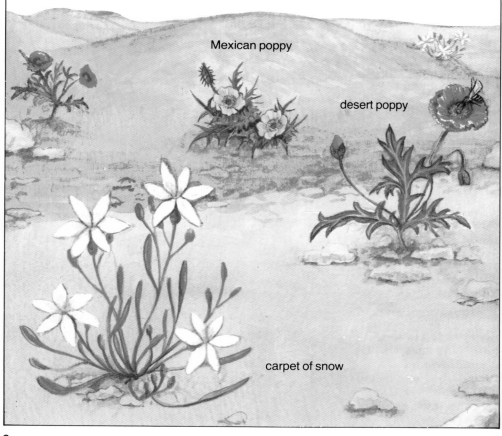

Mexican poppy

desert poppy

carpet of snow

Prickles and spines

Many desert plants have stems which are tough and leathery on the outside but juicy inside. They store water in order to stay alive. These plants are called succulents. The best known ones are cactus plants. Many kinds of cactus are found in the American deserts. Instead of leaves, cactus plants have sharp spines. These lose less water than leaves, and also protect the plants from animals. Some birds nest in cactus stems.

saguaro cactus

barrel cactus

aloe

The ship of the desert

Many animals have adapted to a life in the desert. The best known are the camels. The dromedary, or Arabian camel, has short hair and a single hump. The hump contains reserves of fat, to help it survive where grazing is poor. Camels can go for six days without a drink, and travel long distances in great heat. The Bactrian camel of the cold Asian deserts has two humps and a shaggy coat. For thousands of years camels have been used to carry goods across the desert (below). Long lines of camels travel in groups called caravans.

Big ears

The fennec fox (right) lives in the Sahara. It is the smallest of all foxes, being only 40 centimetres long. Its huge ears increase the surface area of the body and so help it lose heat. Its silky coat also helps it to keep cool. The fennec fox spends the day in a cool burrow, and comes out to hunt by night. It feeds on lizards, snakes, insects and spiders.

Creatures of the sands

The dune cricket (right) is found in Africa's Namib Desert. It has strange feet which prevent it from sinking in the soft sand. Its colour helps it to stay hidden, or camouflaged, against the sand. Insects are hardy creatures, and many have adapted to a life in the desert. Spiders and scorpions also live in deserts. Scorpions have a sting which can kill.

Spot the monster

Reptiles are ideally suited to desert conditions. Many, such as rattlesnakes, are venomous. Their bite is poisonous. The Gila monster (below) is a venomous lizard which is well camouflaged. It is a burrow dweller which feeds on bird eggs and small creatures, and it can survive long periods without eating. Its bite can kill humans. Rattlesnakes and Gilas are found in American deserts.

Hunters of the Kalahari

Some San people of the Kalahari Desert still live by hunting animals. Here, they are collecting grubs. They use these to mix up a poison which they then smear on their arrow tips.

People of the veil

The Tuareg live in the mountains of the southern Sahara. Their name means 'People of the veil'. The men wear blue robes and long black or blue scarves wrapped around their faces. Traditionally, the Tuareg lived by caravan trading and by robbing travellers.

The Aborigines of Australia

The Aborigines lived in Australia for many thousands of years before settlers arrived from Europe. They lived by gathering berries and roots, and hunting animals such as kangaroos. Hunting weapons included the famous boomerang. On the left, an Aborigine is decorating a wooden shield. Although many Aborigines no longer follow the traditional way of life, many remain experts at desert survival. They can find their way across trackless wastes in terrible heat. They know where to find water.

The Bedouin

Many desert people are nomads. They have no settled homes, but wander with their herds. In some parts of some deserts, the rainy seasons produce enough pasture for sheep and goats to graze. The Bedouin live in the deserts of North Africa and the Middle East. Many are still nomads, living in tents made of goat or camel hair. The hair is spun into yarn (right) and woven. The Bedouin are Moslems, so the women wear veils.

Travelling tents

Many desert nomads live in tents made of cloth or skins. Some Kurds live in the hot deserts of Iraq. Their tents are lined with beautiful carpets.

Yurts of the Gobi

Many of the Mongol people who live in the Gobi Desert still live in round tents called yurts (right). These are covered in felt to keep in the warmth during the bitterly cold winter. Originally, the yurts were moved from place to place with the herds. Many yurts are now set up in permanent settlements.

Huts of grass

The San people of the Kalahari Desert often make shelters of branches thatched with long, coarse grass (right). In the dry climate, simple huts can provide adequate shelter and shade. They can be rebuilt when the people move on in search of plants, fruit and game. This group of San is stretching an antelope skin in front of their hut. They sell skins in order to buy other goods, or use them to make cloaks for the women or loin cloths for the men.

Buildings and towns

Not all desert peoples are nomads. Permanent settlements including towns and cities are to be found in many deserts. A common building material is mud, shaped into bricks and dried in the sun. In the American deserts this building style is known as adobe. Famous desert cities include Timbuktu in Mali, on the edge of the Sahara, and Mecca, the holy city of Islam, which is in the Arabian Desert.

Desert buildings (left) often have thick walls and small windows with shutters. These keep the rooms shaded and cool. Many desert houses are built aroud shady courtyards.

Faith in the wilderness

This camel driver (left) faces Mecca in order to pray. He is a Moslem. The desert has inspired many of the world's great religions. The Jewish faith was founded by tribes who lived in the desert for long periods. Jesus Christ went into the desert to pray. The prophet Mohammed, the founder of Islam, also prayed in the desert. American Indians and Australian Aborigines have their own desert religions.

Desert pastimes

The Saudi Arabian on the right is holding a falcon. It is trained to hunt small birds and mammals in the desert. The falconer wears a glove to protect his left hand from the sharp claws, or talons, of the falcon. The falcon wears a hood which is removed for flight. Falconry, which was popular in Europe hundreds of years ago, is still practised in the Arabian Desert.

Other traditional pastimes are also still to be seen. Camels are specially bred for racing. They compete over short distances, and whilst travelling can keep up speeds of 20 kilometres per hour for a whole day.

Trade and markets

Desert peoples have visited this market in Morocco for hundreds of years. They come to buy fruit, vegetables, spices and, today, manufactured goods and suppies.

Many of the world's main trading routes had to cross the deserts before the age of air transport. Camel caravans crossing the Sahara Desert carried salt, gold and ivory. Caravans crossing the deserts of central Asia carried tea, silks, spices and fine carpets. In the last century, the American deserts were crossed by traders and miners in search of gold.

The modern world

Today, the modern way of life is affecting even the peoples who live in remote deserts. This woman may be visited by a doctor (left) once or twice a year. Health care and schooling are now available in most countries. However the way of life has not always improved. It becomes harder and harder to' live by herding or trading. Many desert peoples are very poor.

17

Mining in the desert

This huge truck is tipping bauxite into a crusher. Bauxite is a metal-bearing rock, or ore, used to make aluminium. It is mined in the deserts of Australia. In recent years more and more riches have been discovered beneath the wasteland and baking rocks of the world's great deserts. Phosphates are mined in the Sahara region, to make fertilizers. Chile's Atacama Desert, one of the harshest landscapes on Earth, has copper, iron ore and nitrates. Desert mining has created wealth for some, but rarely for the peoples living there.

Diamonds in the dust

Precious metals such as gold, silver and platinum are to be found in the Australian, American and central Asian deserts. They are used for industry and to make jewellery and coins. Precious and semi-precious stones are also mined in desert regions. The miner (left) is looking for opals in the Australian Desert. He must break through hard rocks to find them. Diamonds are found in the Kalahari and Namib deserts of south-western Africa.

Rigs in the desert

Rigs for drilling natural gas and oil (left) are a familiar sight in many deserts. The Sahara and the Arabian and Iranian deserts produce more oil than anywhere else in the world. The oil lies deep beneath the ground. It was formed millions of years ago from the remains of tiny plants and animals.

Black gold

The oil from desert fields is raised and piped over the desert to refineries, where it is processed. The world has a never-ending need for oil, which is used as fuel and to make plastics. Many countries which produce oil have become rich. For this reason oil is sometimes called 'black gold'. The states around the Arabian desert have become very wealthy. Arab falconers (below) can now travel out into the desert in Mercedes and Land Rovers instead of on the backs of camels.

Desert driving

Driving through the desert can be very dangerous. Very often there is no hard surface. Drivers must follow tyre tracks in the sand (right). They may become stuck in soft dunes, and have to dig their vehicle free. If they become lost, the great heat of the desert soon takes its toll. Extra supplies of food and water must be carried. Heat and rough driving can use up 40 per cent more fuel than normal. Vehicles often form convoys, so that if one driver breaks down, the others can help.

A clear route

Where there are proper roads, they may become covered by drifting sands. Shrubs may be planted along the roadside (left). When they grow, they will act as a barrier. Roads across the Sahara are marked by beacons, so that the route to follow is clear.

Trucking it

Few buses and trains cross deserts, although there are some famous exceptions, such as the railway line from Wadi Halfa to Khartoum in the Sudan. This carries passengers through one of the hottest regions on Earth. Most desert travellers rely on trucks (right) to take them from one oasis to the next. They pay a fare to the driver. Riding on the back of a truck is very dusty and hot. Passengers must shade themselves and cover their faces.

Take the road train

One good thing about driving in the desert is that there is little traffic! In Australia heavy trucks haul long series of trailers, known as road trains, over straight, empty desert roads. This road train (left) is taking cattle to market. It throws up a plume of dust as it speeds along. Journeys can take several days. Driving over such long distances can be exhausting.

Desert herders

This Fulani herdsman lives on the southern edge of the Sahara, in the belt of land known as the Sahel. Raising cattle in such areas can be a hard life. There is only just enough grass and water to support the herds. If the rains fail, many cattle may die. Sometimes the rains fail year after year.

Other livestock raised in desert regions include sheep, goats and camels. They can eat scrub and poor vegetation, and are found in both hot and cold deserts. Yaks are raised in the cold deserts of central and eastern Asia. These are tough mountain oxen with shaggy coats. Yaks provide milk and transport.

Raising cattle

At first sight, the picture on the left looks as if it has been taken in northern Europe. There are green fields and a herd of Friesian cows. However if you look on the horizon, you will see that this is the Arabian Desert. Water is being sprayed on to the fields to irrigate them. The cows are provided with shelters to keep off the heat of the sun. Such modern methods of raising livestock may work well, but they are far too expensive to carry out on a large scale. They rely on a good supply of piped water.

Water for crops

In desert areas, crops cannot be grown without irrigation. The method on the right has been used in Egypt for over 4000 years, and may still be seen today. A bucket called a shaduf is used to raise water from the river. The bucket is attached to a weighted lever, made from a branch. The bucket is pulled below the water. The weight on the lever acts as a balance and pulls the full bucket up again. The water can then be poured from the bucket on to the growing crops. Today, electric pumps may be used to raise river water so that it flows into a network of irrigation channels.

Digging wells for farms

Where there are underground pockets of water, they can be tapped by drilling wells. Sometimes the water forces its own way up to the surface. Sometimes the water is raised by pumps. These may be worked by windmills (left). These kinds of water sources are known as Artesian wells, because they were first dug at Artois, in France. The wells provide water for crops and cattle in deserts and dry lands.

Irrigation the modern way

Major rivers are often dammed in order to provide water for irrigation. The Nile in Egypt, the Colorado in the USA, and the Murray in Australia, are all made use of in this way. The water is piped to desert areas and sprinkled on to the fields by machines. Some of these may move up and down, watering a strip (right). Some crops are watered by hosepipes laid on the ground. Small holes in the pipe release a steady trickle of water near each root. Too much watering can create problems. Salts may be washed out of the soil and rocks, so that the plants cannot grow well. Large irrigation projects may affect the climate, vegetation and wildlife of the area.

Greening the desert

The desert on the left is scorched by the sun and swept by winds. No plants grow here naturally. Yet in the distance green patches can be seen. These circles have been irrigated and sown with hardy wheat. In some countries, such as Israel and Australia, irrigation projects have already made the desert green. In many other countries there is a desperate need to make use of wasteland, but there is not enough money to develop the irrigation schemes that are needed to do this.

Crops for the heat

Even if there is enough water, many crops will not grow in great heat. Traditional oasis crops such as melons, dates and figs will always thrive. Plants such as the jojoba bean may be grown, to provide oil. Scientists have also developed new tough, heat-resistant breeds of crops such as tomatoes (below).

Water from the sea?

Salty, or brackish, water is of no use for irrigating crops. Much of the water raised from wells in the desert is brackish, as it has taken in salts from rocks underground. In the same way, the salt from sea water would kill plants if it were to be used for irrigation. Salt can be removed from sea water at special 'desalination' plants (left). The fresh water produced is used for the irrigation of crops. However the process is expensive and can rarely be used on a large scale.

When the desert spreads

Many of the world's deserts are growing. The Sahara is spreading southwards into the semi-desert region of the Sahel. The Gobi too is in danger of moving southwards towards the Great Wall of China. The Chinese are planting a 'great green wall' of trees in order to stop farm land being eroded into desert. The climate may help deserts spread. Long periods without rain may kill plants in surrounding areas.

Often, it is humans that make the desert spread. Herds of goats will destroy trees (above). Over-grazing can turn whole landscapes into wasteland (right). The clearing of forests for firewood or for farming allows soil to be washed or blown away. In the 1930s land in the USA was overfarmed and stripped of trees. Good farmland was soon turned into a 'dustbowl'.

Drought and famine

The Sahel region often goes for long periods without rainfall. During these periods of drought, water holes may dry up completely (left). Millions of cattle may die. Many people starve and there is a famine. People become ill and weak, and many die. As farmland turns to desert, people leave their homes and wander in search of food and medical help. Many set up camps on the edges of cities, but fail to find food or work. People from the richer countries of the world often send food and medical aid to help people who are starving.

What can be done

Emergency food supplies can save lives in the short term. In the long term, ways of farming must be changed. Trees must be planted to prevent soil erosion. Stoves must burn less firewood. Projects must be started to save water. The right crops must be planted, and overgrazing prevented.

Lessons of the past

The Tassili Mountains are in south-west Algeria, in the middle of the Sahara Desert. Today, the area is a burnt-out wilderness. However 10 000-year-old rock paintings found in the mountains (left) show that long ago cattle grazed this area. Other Saharan paintings confirm that the desert was once green and fertile. Perhaps it was over-grazing and the cutting down of trees that originally turned the region into desert. If so, could it not be green once again?

Crops for the future

Sorghum (below) is a hardy grain crop which needs little water to grow. It thrives in hot countries and is cultivated in the lands around the Sahara. Today scientists have made sorghum produce far better crops than ever before. It is plants like this which will become widely grown if the world's deserts are to be farmed in the future.

Growing without soil

We now know how to grow crops in spacecraft far above the Earth. Surely we can work out a system of growing food in desert areas? Hydroponics (right) is the science of growing plants without soil. Plants can be grown indoors, in a mixture of water and chemicals. Poor soil and a harsh climate need no longer be a problem. However hydroponics is a very expensive way of farming, and relies on a supply of piped water. Desert lands need a cheaper and more basic way of producing food, which uses more traditional methods.

Desert industries

Mount Isa (left) is near Simpson Desert in Queensland, Australia. It is one of the many mining towns in the Australian Desert. In future years the world's deserts are going to be made use of more and more for mining and industry. Desert peoples who have traditionally lived by herding or hunting will become miners or factory workers. As our planet becomes more and more crowded, every bit of space will have to be used. New cities may grow up around the new industries. There will be no shortages of sunshine, and this could be turned into electricity to provide power for homes. Underground houses could be built which would stay cool. Let us hope however that thousands of years from now some deserts still survive with their empty spaces and their own grim beauty.

Index

The numbers in **bold** are illustrations.

Aborigines 13, **13,** 16
adobe 15
Africa 2, 8, 11, 13
America 2, 8, 11, 17, 24, 26
antelope skins 15
Asia 2, 17
Australia 2, 13, 18, 21, 24, 29

beacons 20
Bedouin 13, **13**
birds 9

cacti 7, 9, **9**
  barrel 9
  saguaro 9
camels 3, 10, **16,** 22
  Bactrian 3, **3,** 10, **10**
  caravans 10, 17
  drivers 16, **16**
  dromedary 10
  racing 16
cattle 22, **22,** 23, 27, 28, **28**
cold deserts 2, 3, 14
Colorado, River 5, 24

date palms 6, **6**
desalination plants 25, **25**
deserts 2, 14, 18
  Atacama 2, 18
  Arabian 2, 15, 16, 19, 22
  Australian 2, 18, **18**
  cold 2
  Death Valley 3, **3**
  Gobi 2, 3, 14, 26
  Great American 2, 5, **5,** 8, 11
  Iranian 19

Kalahari 2, 12, 15, 18
Kara Kum 2, **2**
Namib 2, 11, 18
Sahara 2, **2,** 3, 10, 12, 15, 17, 18, 19, 20, 22, 26, 28
Simpson 29
Thar 2, 7
diamonds 18
drilling 19, **19**
drought 27
dune crickets 11, **11**
dunes 4, **4,** 20
dustbowls 26

Egypt 2, 6, 24
erosion 5

faith 16
falconry 16, **16,** 19, **19**
fennec fox 10, **10**
flash floods 5
Fulani 22, **22**

goats 22, 26, **26**
Grand Canyon 5
Great Wall of China 26

health care 17
herding 17, 22, **22,** 29
hunting 29
huts 15, **15**
hydroponics 29, **29**

India 7
industries 29, **29**
insects 10, 11

irrigation 6, 23, **23,** 24-25, **24**
Israel 24

Jesus Christ 16

Kurds 14, **14**

lizards 10, 11
  Gila monster 11, **11**

Mecca 16
mining 18, 29
Mohammed 16
Mongols 14
Moslems 13
mountains 4
Mount Isa 29, **29**
Murray, River 24

Nile, River 6, **6,** 24
nomads 13, 14

oases 6, **6,** 7, 21, 25
overfarming 26
overgrazing 27, 28

plants 7, 8-9, 25, **25,** 26, 29
  flowering 8, **8**
  shrubs 20, **20**
  sorghum 28, **28**
  succulents 9, **9**

quartz 4

railways 21
rainfall 3, 4, 5, 8, 22

road trains 21, **21**

Sahel 26, 27
San 7, **7,** 12, **12,** 15, **15**
sand 2, 4, 5, 6, 8
schooling 17
scorpions 11
shadufs 23
sheep 22, **26**
Sinai Peninsula 2
snakes 10, 11
  rattlesnakes 11
spiders 10, 11
springs 6, 7
storms 5

Tassili Mountains 28
temperatures 2, 3
tents 13, 14, **14**
trading 17
trees 8, 27
  acacias 8
  Joshua 8
  thorns 8
trucks 21
Tuareg 12, **12**

underground houses 29

wadis 5, **5**
water holes 7, **7,** 27, **27**
wells 6, 7, 23, 25
  Artesian 23, **23**

yaks 22
yurts 14, **14**

HEINEMANN CHILDREN'S REFERENCE
a division of Heinemann Educational Books Ltd
Halley Court, Jordan Hill, Oxford OX2 8EJ

OXFORD LONDON EDINBURGH
MELBOURNE SYDNEY AUCKLAND
MADRID ATHENS BOLOGNA
SINGAPORE IBADAN NAIRBOI HARARE
GABORONE KINGSTON PORTSMOUTH NH(USA)

ISBN 0 431 00931 7

A CIP catalogue record for this book
is available from the British Library

© Heinemann Educational Books Ltd 1990
First published 1990

Design by Julian Holland Publishing Ltd
Cover concept by Groom and Pickerill

Printed in Hong Kong

90 91 92 93 94 95 10 9 8 7 6 5 4 3 2 1

Acknowledgements
Illustrations: BLA Publishing Limited.
Photographs: *a = above m = middle b = below*
2*a* ZEFA; 2*b* Peter Scoones/Seaphot; 3*a* ZEFA; 3*b* The Hutchison Library; 4 Hans Christian Heap/
Seaphot; 5*a* ZEFA; 5*b* The Hutchison Library; 6*a* Douglas Dickens; 6*b*, 7*a* ZEFA; 7*b* Peter Johnson/
NHPA; 10*a* ZEFA; 10*b* Peter Johnson/NHPA; 11*a* Anthony Bannister/NHPA; 11*b* Stephen Kraseman/
NHPA; 12*a* Peter Johnson/NHPA; 12*b*, 13*a*, 13*b* The Hutchison Library; 14*a* South American Pictures;
14*b* ZEFA; 15*a* Peter Johnson/NHPA; 15*b* ZEFA; 16*a*, 16*b* The Hutchison Library; 17*a* Mike Coltman/
Seaphot; 17*b* The Hutchison Library; 18*a* Chris Fairclough; 18*b* The Hutchison Library; 19*a* British
Petroleum; 19*b* The Hutchison Library; 20*a*, 20*b*, 21*a*, 21*b* ZEFA; 22*a*, 22*b*, 23*a*, 23*b* The Hutchison
Library; 24*a*, 24*b* Hans Christian Heap/Seaphot; 25*a* The Hutchison Library; 25*b* British Petroleum; 26*a*
Dennis Firminger/Seaphot; 26*b* Hans Christian Heap/Seaphot; 27*a* Jeremy Hartley/Oxfam; 27*b* Oxfam;
28*a*, 28*b* The Hutchison Library; 29*a* I.C.I. Plant Protection; 29*b* The Hutchison Library.